Color My Botanicals
Coloring Book
Volume I

By Jinah Park-Kennedy
Copyright © 2016
ISBN-13: 987-1533162304

Color My Botanicals
Coloring Book
Volume 1

By Jinah Park-Kennedy
Copyright © 2016 by Jinah Park-Kennedy
ISBN-13: 987-1533162304
ISBN-10: 1533162301

Dear Fellow Colorer,

Thank you for purchasing COLOR MY BOTANICALS
Coloring Book, Volume 1.
I really enjoyed drawing all the images here in this book,
I hope you enjoy just as much coloring them.
I love flowers so much. I started drawing flowers and foliages
because both my son and my husband suffer from seasonal
allergies. Since I cannot bring real flowers into our house,
I just started coloring books with flowers in them. Then I
started drawing my own flowers to color, which lead to
creating this coloring book.

Studio Decompress© is what I call a corner of my house
where I don't clean and nothing is in order. I can sit and draw
or color or just read to decompress from general pressures
of everyday life. I am very lucky to have a space as such (many
thanks to my generous husband who understands and my son
who can keep himself well occupied). Creating this book and
finding time and space for it was joyous and productive for me.
I think it is rare to find joy & productivity in life - as why I am
truly grateful at this time in my life.
Thank you for purchasing this book, and I hope for you the best.
Jinah
2016

ISBN-13: 978-1533162304
ISBN-10: 1533162301

Fellow Colorist,

On the left side of the pages in this book, I purposely did not place an image to color. I thought it could be best used to doodle, write notes, add random thoughts, lists and reminders. Also the paper is sort of on the thin side, so it's best only one side of the pages are used to color. I personally love layering with just plain color pencils. Sometimes I would accent an area with ballpoint pens, gel pens and even spots of marker to give it a bit of depth.

And speaking of color pencils, there so many brands to choose from in the market. In my experiences, the lesser expensive ones are best if you are looking for a paler finish, or a pastel color palette and more subtle transitions. The artist qualities are best for gradient fields and spots of pure color. The lesser expensive color pencils are mixed more of fillers (extra wax, clay, etc) than actual color pigments, while the artist brands are softer, deeper colors from the excess of real pigments in the leads. And to this mix of material matters, there is also the hands of the colorists. Some color solid, some like to layer in and work up to a solid field of color. It is not only the materials that can affect the final effect, but the hands of the colorer.

In all, I am happy to color and share. But I am even happier that you have bought my coloring book. All the images are hand drawn and flowed out from my head to my hand. Because none of the images were made through a computer software, there are more variances with the lines, and a whole natural sketch qualities will be noticiable. What I have notice when I colored them, a painterly feel will shine through since the lines and images are hand drawn. Some might want a more polished line to color within--and might find this book alittle too erratic, some will find solace in the natural feel of the lines as they are coloring in them, randomly running all over the place. Sometimes the line are so unperfect, it can push you out or take you in further to the ideas of just being in it.

As much as I love to color, I love to just draw. What a wonderful time it is when a simple thing as drawing and coloring can be something to look forward to and share. Til the next Volume in my series......

Jinah.

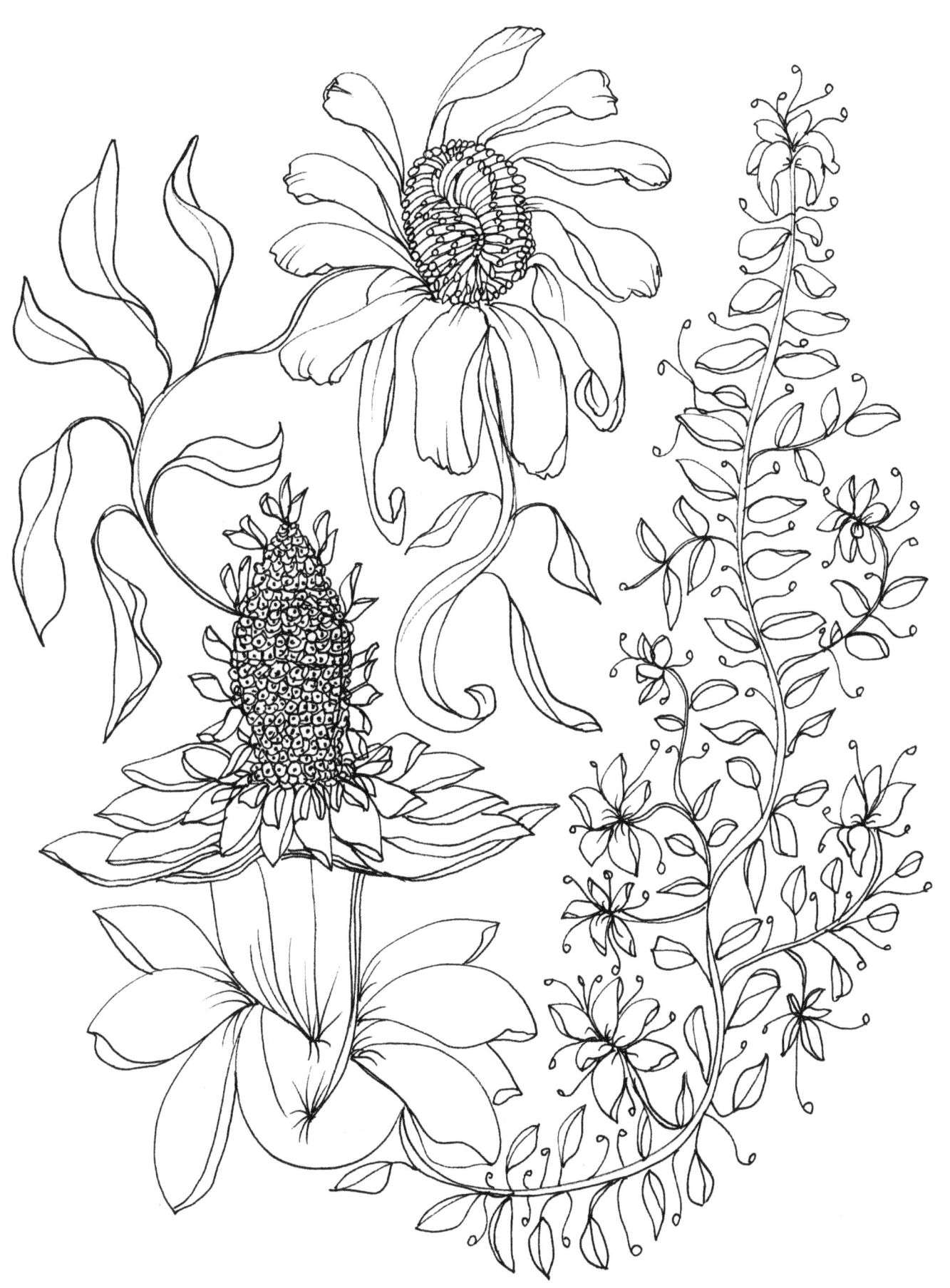

Thank You

Thank You so much for purchasing my 1st Coloring Book.
Thank You also to my family
for their forever support in anything that I do.
Happy Coloring! ;)